EDITOR-IN-CHIEF
Alan Fox

EDITOR
Timothy Green

LOGO DESIGN
David Navas

ASSISTANT EDITOR
Megan Green

COVER ART
kerry rawlinson
"Whirling," 2019

EDITOR EMERITUS
Stellasue Lee

PROOFREADING
Jeffrey Gerretse

© 2021 by The Rattle Foundation

Rattle Young Poets Anthology, 2021

www.Rattle.com

CONTENTS

2021

Note on the Cover Artist

Decades ago, kerry rawlinson wanted to be a ballerina. An autodidact and bloody-minded optimist, she gravitated from sunny Zambian skies to solid Canadian soil, and now dances with words and images, with contradictions and synchronicities, still barefoot. She photographs extensively, then dabbles with various digital tools to develop and move each piece. She never uses Photoshop, and often enhances pieces with acrylics. Her granddaughter Emma is the Whirler.

kerryrawlinson.tumblr.com

Rattle Young Poets Anthology
Guidelines

1) Poems may be submitted by the poet, or the poet's parent, legal guardian, or teacher. Teachers may only submit on behalf of up to five students per year.

2) The author of the poem must have been age 15 or younger when the poem was written, and 18 or younger when submitted.

3) The poets may use their whole name, first name, or a pseudonym at their parents' discretion. We will not publish any contact information.

4) Submit up to four poems at a time.

5) Upon acceptance, a parent or legal guardian must sign a release allowing us to publish the poem. We will also request an audio recording of the poem by the child for inclusion in the ebook version and/or on our website.

6) Submissions will only be accepted through our Submittable portal. Include the parent/guardian's name and mailing address, and the child's age when the poems were written. The link to the portal can be found at:

www.rattle.com/children

Annual Deadline:
November 15th

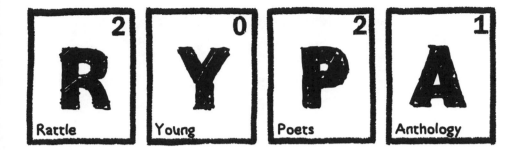

Maria Arango

¿IDENTITY?

El presidente Donal Trump said
they're bringing drugs. They're bringing crime. They're rapists.

My brown sugar skin delicately
compresses me with warmth
as I try to understand the
anatomy of my body.

I close my eyes,
hearing the melody of my melanin
drowning into
a force adaptation.

And he said
they're bringing drugs. They're bringing crime. They're rapists.

I grasp to my woven tan threads,
holding the warmth of my color—
because that's what keeps me safe.

I was born in the green mountains of Colombia
with bright blue skies and with
the sparkly eyes of people
who never stop smiling.
The happiest population in the world.
And I grew in the land
of dreams; of dreamers
where the air is full of possibilities, posibilidades like *mama* said.

America was where I saw mama y papa
work hard to make a home for me.
I thought I knew where I was from.
But
they're bringing drugs. They're bringing crime. They're rapists.

And in that moment

[...]

honey began to drip
from my eyes to my café colombiano.
I lost my location
because he said
they're bringing drugs. They're bringing crime. They're rapists.

So I tried to translate
the recipes of arroz con leche.
Is it rice first and then milk,
or milk first and then rice?
I know how to make an apple pie
but I do not know how to make an empanada.

And after some conversation with familia that I haven't met,
and fake laughs
over jokes I couldn't understand,
after not being Latina enough.

He still said
they're bringing drugs. They're bringing crime. They're rapists.

Being Latina in America
is what I held onto.

But I was a misplaced check mark
where being Latina wasn't a race
or an identity but a fear.

So, I continued to write in English,
and every time it's like I'm
floating on the surface of the ocean,
but I sink five feet further as I lose
my Spanish palabra por palabra stanza by stanza.

And so he says
they're bringing drugs. They're bringing crime. They're rapists.

The sun wraps me with hunger,
holding onto the particles of my identity.
In the reflection of water,

the one we cross
for a better tomorrow.
Reflects upon my brown skin a
battlefield of a war
of natives and Europeans.
And in that moment, I knew:

we are dancing bodies of bones and flesh swimming
to an unknown race,
an unknown race carrying
the world within our touch.

We are from the same soil
where trees flourish,
we are the sun
holding our warmth.

We are the world in history.

As papá said
porque somos humanos,
estamos conectados.
Somos unos.
We are one. Connected

I'm not bringing drugs. I bring mama y papa

I'm not bringing crime. I give America my cultura

I'm not a rapist. I'm a brown student

Mi nombre es

inmigrante.

Matthew Burk

THE ROLLER COASTER

The day I rode
a roller coaster
for the first time

it seemed like fun

but then
it went upside down

and I was terrified

like I might
break into a billion pieces
onto the ground

and my atoms
would swell the earth
bending space and time

and the past would fall into the present.

Natalia Chepel

SEMANTICS

There is some meaning to the word semantics
It's why *b a n a n a* means yellow fruit
A beeping box is called "computer,"
A pencil's a utensil
And keys are something that you lose

But now you see, thanks to the thoughts of some romantics
I drink from a glass glass, and watch a fly fly
Then in the fall, when the leaves leave the trees
And I hear "duck!"—I duck, but nevermind
It was just a goose

Why is it then, that there's one meaning to the word "semantics"?
It seems in all their antics, those hopeless romantics
Have all forgot about
"Semantics"—see a man tick, just like a bomb about to blow
Although he's patient, his roommate's tics have managed, finally,

To light his fuse.

Melissa Alma Di Martino

SAIVE ME BY THES WENDROUS

Saive me by thes wendrous
and this per of lo, and below
me, all my life i immagin
ther faises, and if i now
them and then they well never
no me, not obof them, and
part of them

Natalie Friis

PAPER PEOPLE

If there was a paper me
And there was a paper you,
We would be paper people
With a new point of view.

Paper people would be fragile
A wrong grasp would cause a tear.
Paper people would be so light
The breeze could blow them anywhere.

Paper people would be simple
Their skin plain and white
But paper people would give paper cuts
That wouldn't bleed quite right.

Money would be paper too
It would still be thin and green
But somehow more important
Than the paper people's needs.

The paper people
Need a paper economy
And with the paper empire
Comes paper poverty.

Paper people would always find a way
To fold into paper airplanes
In order to escape
From the paper people's brains.

Even in a paper world
Paper people are ripped apart
The only way to love people
Is to love a paper person's heart.

Paul Ghatak

COUNTING TO ONE

It's really easy counting to one.
The moment you start, you're already done.

Grant

LIONS ROAR

I like lions
      their manes, that they're shaggy like sheep's wool.
I like that they're the boss of the jungle.
They tell the animals what to do kind of nicely,
      but kind of with a down voice that is calm
      like water in a pond.

Kevin Gu

THE YANGTZE

i.
The first time I dipped my toes in the Yangtze my mother
told me the story of Qu Yuan, a great poet
who drowned himself
along the branching twines of the river.
I laughed at her, split-grinned,
and submerged my legs anyway.
Later that night, I dreamt
of jasmine rice and zongzi.

ii.
Indigo means immensity. Mother cooked 麻婆豆腐 (*Mapo Tofu*) for me
when the winters were still long—the middle
stages of twilight at 5 PM. The rusty heater pumped
rivulets of smoky air,
scent lingering in my lungs like yinghua syrup.
Her calloused fingertips kneaded
my fleshy face while the rest of the world was quiet,
only us alone in the house.

iii.
Mouth gaping under the light-year skies. Taste
the moon's perspiration, it tells me. It grips me.
They all want something,
the Yangtze said to me that day.
Mother stroked my burnt hair,
blackened soot on the thin skin of my undereyes.
Find yourself in the infinite
or it will drive you under
the currents.

iv.
The silky black felt frozen between my toes,
Chang Jiang was its other name. Mother told me
it meant long river. Long falling, long gone.
Fish nipped on peach-frosted skin as inward legs

held the weight of the horizon. The listless sky spun around
two axes, one centered above me another piercing
my side, asymmetric, indigo split like gears
grinding flaked sugar stars. My chest trembled,
eyes closed at the sight of the undertow.

Why did Qu Yuan drown himself?

The Yangtze answered, over
and over and over:

He yearned for the sky
and found the next closest thing.

Kakul Gupta

TEN HAIKU

metropolitan city—
each raga
smoke-laden

coin collection—
the clink
of grandma's voice

away from home—
the crackle
of mother's onions

virtual classroom—
now my friends
captured in squares

gas tragedy—
pale glow
of the sun

winter fog
... with each layer
a brewing argument

winter chill ...
in search of bread
a roaming dog

sunrise
the old city
lights up

summer holidays—
mangoes
in my dreams

winter fog ...
each tree
a ghost

Maria Gil Harris

LIKE MAGIC

The sand aflame,
I walked towards the sleeping ocean.

I held my breath, despite the snorkel resting on my dried lips,
As I swam to the endless horizon.

Thousands of fish scurrying away from me,
My heavy strokes shattering the surface of the water.

At last, I lay still,
In hopes of catching a glimpse of their sky blue scales.

Just as fast as they had swum away, they returned,
Bubbles rising from their fins, rushing to pop at the surface.

They began sifting through my fingers,
Disappearing at every curve.

Like ballerinas in blue,
They danced around, leaving a trail of light behind them.

Many times I have tried to recreate that moment,
But I have discovered that magic does not repeat itself.

Adrianna Ho

PASTA SANDWICHES IN QUARANTINE

1.

In quarantine
I missed my uncle's wedding
because it was cancelled in May,

and Take Your Child to Work Day:
I was going to meet my mom's coworkers and friends
and join her meetings.

I missed Field Day with games, and May Day with
carnival games. Mr. C., my gym teacher, had planned it,
and you could get half a lemon with a candy straw!

I miss going to school.
I miss having sleepovers: one in the beginning of summer
and one at the end.

Some of my friends couldn't come
to my birthday party. The magician
couldn't come.

Before quarantine, I had plans
with my good friend who moved to Boston
to get together and sell all the leftover candies

and save every penny.

2.

In quarantine
I turned 8
and learned to ride a bike

[...]

I learned that daddy makes yummy sandwiches
and mommy makes good pasta.
Pasta sandwiches for lunch!

I still can see
my ballet friends
and classmates right online.

I still pick flowers on nature walks
and walk on the rocks
to get over the streams.

In quarantine, I grew half an inch.
I learned how to feed my dog Rusty
and take him outside.

I learned how to type without looking at the keyboard
and how to make
peanut butter sandwiches when daddy is busy, and

that our school nurse is a good yoga instructor
and our second grade teacher reminds me
that if I believe I can, I can.

I learned that I don't have to go out to the theater
because I can watch movies at my house
cuddling, eating snacks, and petting Rusty.

I learned I can relax anytime and anywhere,
I close my eyes, I take deep breaths
A couple of minutes later I open my eyes

and put my hands on my heart, and namaste.
I learned to read chapter books: *Harry Potter,*
The Lion, The Witch and the Wardrobe, oh! And don't forget

Charlie and the Chocolate Factory!
I learned to organize my closet, to keep it clean.
I grew to wear my big sister's clothes while in quarantine.

I learned that the crown-shaped virus is the Coronavirus.
If I could talk to the Coronavirus,
I'd say, "The Heat Is On! I Know

The Heat Can Stop You From Spreading."

Emma Hoff

THE WEIGHT OF THE HEAVENS

Was the minotaur
Really
A monster?

Or was he
Just placed here
To scare mankind.

Like Atlas,
Who was placed here to live,
Instead bearing everything,
The heavens.

What were the heavens like,
I wonder,
And would the minotaur like it there?

Would it be easier
If you were served by a servant,
Who holds you up?

Or would you take pity,
For Atlas already
Holds enough.

But how much would the heavens weigh,
If there were
No people?

Does it matter how many people
Are there,
For each person adds just a little weight.

Surely the stars weigh more,
Or say,
The moon?
And surely the sun burns
Atlas's already weighted
Shoulders.

Or maybe,
The grief
That he isn't out there doing things.

The minotaur is.

Ivy Hoffman

ONLY DAYS BEFORE LEAVING FOR COLLEGE, I NOTE THE EXISTENCE OF MY BROTHER

I.

My brother sits in the corner
With his papers all around,
And he is drawing.

He does not listen
To our conversations.
You will only see his foot tap,
Sometimes, when we play Wings,

And then you will know
He is real.

Sometimes I think
He is drawing me,
Though he tries to throw me off,
He never looks up
From his paper,

But when I smile, I see him,
Though he shields his face
With his knees, smile.

He never speaks to me.
Before I go to bed, I pray
That God will bless my brother
With speech.

When I dance in the living room,
My face looking up at the ceiling fan,
And no further, with my arms
Spread wide, my legs kicking
Sporadically and wonderfully,

My brother draws, and taps his foot,
And I know he's dancing with me,
In his own way, he is pushing music
From the tip of his charcoal pencil.

II.

And now I am venturing out
Into the beautiful and terrifying world,
No longer will I be safe
Within these strong brick walls,
I will only have myself.

And my brother will remain here,
He does not know the bright colors
Of the universe, he will only know
The musty darkness of his charcoal.

Color is a funny thing, I have a
Memory that is not my own,
And it is devoid of color:

My mother, screaming.
I remember later, long after she
Brought me into this world
With glorious triumph, a warrior,

Someone told me
That blood in black and white
Is chocolate sauce—the same
Consistency, the same darkness.

Bone on bone, limbs reaching,
Life: my father sitting in the
Waiting room, he does not
Know me yet, he does not

[...]

Think of me at all,
Only mother, only
Brother.

Life devoid of color,
It is not my memory.

It is not mine to bear.

I was chosen,
Or he was chosen,
God did something
Right or wrong,
God did something.

III.

I do not know what he draws.
Like a dream, I approach
And my brother retreats
Into his corner.

His eyes are green or blue,
I think, they are not dark
And sad like mine, they are
Bright and blameless,

He is uncomplaining.

God did not gift my brother
With speech, he was not
Blessed with life,
Only something like it:

Continuance, habit,
A steady pattern.

I cannot see his face,
It is always behind his knees,
But I know him.

Like I know myself,
As the only thing I am sure of,
My brother's drawings are beautiful,
My brother's voice, I know,
Is beautiful,

My brother, often unobserved,
A shadow in the corner,
Is beautiful.

Jessie Johnson

DURING A LONG DRIVE, I SMELL VINEGAR

and I know your secret, *No, impossible, not again.*
You spit a wad of tobacco into an empty bottle, subtly.
I pretend not to notice. There's a lump in between your cheek,
rotting away your teeth and staining your tongue.

But you spit a wad of tobacco into an empty bottle
and I'm knocked back to 1400 Mahantongo Street,
watching it rot away your teeth and stain your tongue.
Five-year-old-me dumping Skoal into the garbage, disgusted

enough that I'm knocked back to 1983; 3rd Avenue
where your dad died, bronchiole charred from cigarettes.
Five-year-old me spilling Skoal on the couch, panicking
from its stench and mom's face when she'd seen. *Oh God*, she'd say

when you'd remember how your dad died, bronchiole: charred. Fear
made you replace it with sunflower seeds, gum, something to chew,
surrendering its stench and my face when I'd see. *Please God*, I'd pray
when you'd try to quit. I sit in your truck as you side-spit into a bottle,

shocked that you've replaced the sunflower seeds with chew. Again
I pretend not to notice. There's a lump in my throat;
you tried to quit. I sit in silence as you side-spit into a bottle.
I know our secret. *No. Impossible. Not again.*

Dahee Joy Kang

MY NAME

When I was a baby, my name meant
a dedication to God
Dahee meaning Jesus' joy
it meant life
it meant another black-haired baby
in a sea full of black-haired babies
in a country ¾ surrounded by sea
강다희
Kang Dahee
It has a nice ring to it, don't you think?

When I was three, my name meant
unfamiliar letters
on a strange laminated green card
in a foreign country
"Joy," they decided
my name would be Dahee Joy Kang
it meant a quick handing off of the card
from the hands of a bored government worker
to the trembling hands of my parents
and a call for "next!"
welcome to America

When I was in second grade, my name meant
a sudden realization:
that I was different from others
it meant a childish wish for sameness
it meant drawing pictures of girls
with blonde hair
and blue eyes
and paper white skin
scrawling different names on my own paper
with the desperation of an eight-year old wanting to fit in

When I was in fifth grade, my name meant
nervous excitement on our trip to Korea
it meant finally feeling like I belonged
amongst all these people who looked just like me ...
and then suddenly realising that I don't
belong, that is
it meant that
I was too "Dahee" to belong in America
and too "Joy" to belong in Korea
but when I came back
my name meant crying for a week straight anyway
because I missed being able to get lost
in a crowd of people with the same skin as mine

When I was in sixth grade, my name meant
trying to make myself as American as possible
begging my mom to stop packing me kimchi
joking about my small eyes and good grades
it meant laughing
when a white boy told me that my green card
meant my opinion didn't matter
it meant clenching my teeth
as TSA agents assumed I couldn't speak English
it meant watching the Independence Day fireworks with tears
because I wasn't American enough to celebrate

Now that I'm a sophomore, my name means
myself
it means two independence days
it means my ancestors survived
which means so can I
it means I build a meaning for my own names
so that it can mean something new
for every person I meet
Dahee Joy Kang

It has a nice ring to it, don't you think?

Chloe Lin

CULTURED

my first language was not one of
white bread and watching fireworks
burst red white and
blue no my first
language was riding down the
rural streets my arms wrapped
around the waist of my
grandmother speeding on a
motorcycle was pineapple cakes and
bubble tea.

my parents never tried to
americanize
me never tried to add vanilla to
soy milk or replace 巧虎 with
spongebob they didn't want me to forget the
white sun
blue sky
wholly red earth.

i went to this nursery
school that taught in chinese the
teacher was from shanghai spoke with such
definition like slapping someone across the
face i came
home with the same stinging shanghai
accent as i proudly recited:

"凳子"
"勺子"

they stood still the sound of my
slap ringing throughout the
house perhaps that was the first
time they realized they had lost a

part of me to
another country.
i went into
kindergarten not knowing a
speck of english i knew
"yes" i knew
"no" i knew of my english name but did
not know how to write it in the roman
alphabet rather in large chinese
characters no
curves only straight lines down and
right.

in first grade i decided that i
hated my name and changed it to
"olivia" an english name that meant
"olive" in latin a name you type into the google
search bar and all that comes up are pictures of
white blonde women.

my parents never tried to
americanize me because there's a
difference in being an american citizen and
american a difference between representing
stars or the sun i think my parents
believe it's a competition when i'm craving
burgers or listening to justin
bieber but they tend to
forget that

the sun is also a star a
testament to how two
worlds can be so far apart yet collide a
mismatched harmony.

Naomi Ling

FORGIVE ME IF I ASK WHETHER ACTORS FEEL LONELY

The actress on TV   announces,   *we were on a break!*
    and everyone claps. So many beginnings
      culled into a single   punchline. This isn't how it goes
in real life: so many   endings in tired eyes.
    Wednesday.   The boy I love, hanging   from the
    ceiling with ankles blooming red   like wrists.
Bodies   are meant to be displayed. This is a   world
    that forgets   that it's a   world:
Or maybe   it doesn't mind.   *Cry me a river,*
    the actress   is wailing. She's talking   and she isn't
talking. Zipper fraying.   Mouth hemorrhaging.
    I wonder if she   ever feels lonely: the
actress,
I mean. I don't want to mistake her   for   a
    moth-desecrated   streetlight.   I imagine her
turning like violets   in her sleep, remembering   herself only
    when she steps on set.   *I want a world*
for my own, a world that forgets   *my name.*   Silly me.
    I already have one.   Funny how a thousand
faces   can reimagine themselves   as pixels,   how
    it is possible to   cry for someone who is
half-silvered   behind a screen. On the TV,   the
    actress smiles like   Dorothy, like Dolly,
and   martyrs herself to the all-American   housewife.

J

Josephine Miner

I TRAVEL THROUGH THE MOON
as sung to her mother

Yes I go through the places
I go see out into the dark side
I travel through the moon

After I travel through the moon
I go through a tree
And I get stuck and just jump out
I'm not afraid

Then I go through the bushes
And see my house
Where I belong

And after I go through my home
I go into it and say hi
And see my family's heart

Then I go through the jungle
And get inspired by something scary
I say I won't hurt you
I'll be nice to you and stuff

After that I will just go through over the earth
And I'll fly over space
And I'll just go right into God's heart
Into the fire

Then I'll see my friend
And then I'll see my past

And so I travel through the moon
And I never see my destination again
And then I take a right step
For everything I know
And take One. More. Trip. Through the moon.

Mackenzie Munoz

CATCHING DREAMS

Standing on the edge
of a mountain
catching dream after dream.
When I hold them in my hands,
I listen to every one of them.

Perry Sloan

FIERCENESS OF THE NIGHT

The three rhinos standing peacefully in the water
As the lightning flashes
Like thousands of tiny lights formed together
To make one long string of electricity
The whole sky was lit up
And the lightning shined like lights
On a Christmas tree
The trees in the distance were dark silhouettes
Against the brilliant sky
The thousands of rocks joined together on the ground
To make one big rock
And the rhinos still stood patiently
Together against the fierceness of the night
As the wind raged on
And the sky grew dimmer
The rhinos still stood together
Against the fierceness of the night

Hannah Straub

CADILLAC MOUNTAIN

I climbed until my calves caught fire.
I climbed until my braids became a nest.
At the very top, I could see everything.
Blue and green, stained red and orange,
Like blood, and beautiful. I remember
Most the jagged edges, rock slicing
The rubber of my shoes. I did not break,
Though the light threatened to cut me
Into pieces. Shaded eye, golden shoulder.
I worry sometimes that I'm crumbling
Anyway. Whether I'm shards or ashes,
Stones or sand, let me lie in the moss,
Or the gentle spaces in the curves
Of the trees the visitors wear away
With their desperate palms.
Their calloused hands steal the roughness
For themselves, fingers terrified to love
Their own softness, and the ease with which they
May break. Splinter. Shatter. Split.
So they steal, and while I rested there
I remembered that I was the vandal too,
That home is a place I have ruined.
I will remember that it is the only
Space that forgave me.
I blinked open and shut to the world.
No matter where I looked everything
Was distant. The wind chose then to show
How little it cared for me, pushing me
Surely towards the edge as I dug my heels
Into the granite. Though I was not falling
I was stumbling, in the way I clung to people
I could not reach, memories as useless
As the wire guardrails. I held on
To the fragile ties and swallowed the vista,
Eyes desperate, not like a thirst but like

A moment gained, used, wasted—
Wasted in the way that my vulnerability
Was always my first thought. My hands
Were shaking, but what terrified me
Was I wasn't afraid at all. An apparition,
A split second, and I saw my gold wind
And green tears and it felt like a numbness.
The person I knew and didn't understand
Stared back at me and I felt not quite love
But the hollow brink of it. And now, I look
Back in sparse recollection wondering if
The emptiness of that pinnacle knew
How much I had taken as I left it behind.

Ha Trang Tran

A LOVE LETTER FOR HOME

Some day when I make my grand return,
I will take the long way home
on a rusty motorcycle,
passing by time-worn book stores, and French-wounded buildings
in the fresh autumn air, tinged with cheap cigarette butts
    and black cardamom.
I will breathe in the edge nibbled leaves that scatter the streets,
tune into the sizzling sounds of the market,
and confront my eroding mother tongue.
I will dream the dream of calico cats that bask in the twilight sun,
warm as the heat of noon, sweet as iced cà phê sữa.
And when the fire autumn fades, and the world is painted grey,
while the skies stretch further than the abandoned train tracks
that lead to the edge of time,
I will no longer fit the part of the past-girl, and the mirrors won't
    reflect the same way.
The city will still hold me in the creases of her palms
tracing the branches of her Phoenix hands,
singing her nostalgic melodies alley by alley,
bent beneath the roof-tops
that trickle raindrops like tears from daybreak to crepuscule.
Where I come from will never change,
neither on paper nor in creed,
so tattooed on my heart are the memories of Hà Nội.

Shreya Vikram

DIY PROJECT

stage i.

there is a word for looking
into the mirror and not seeing
yourself—tell myself this
daily.

stage ii.

he pretends not to see
me when he takes out my gift. closing his eyes
with his hands, asks darling, where
are you? where is my sweetheart? I don't see
her, no I don't. shake my head then say I'm here and he peeks
through his fingers, forehead wrinkling, asks and who are you now?
I don't know you, no I don't. who are you?

stage iii.

forget old diseases & gather
new ones. stomach aches
unexpectedly. forgotten
pain whips into my age
old bones. time's contrived
as the flesh: in the end,
must remember everything
is something made. must be someone
to do the making. watch my hurried breath
steal away the candles and leave us
gasping.

stage iv.

the final canvas is nameless. slaughter
the s so we can steal a little
happiness for ourselves. take out
the i & leave
it unsigned so it will wander
without a mother like everything else
I love.

Why do you like writing poetry?

Maria Arango: "I write poems because it allows me to connect with others. To be truthful and to realize that in the not-so-good moments, good can arise. Poetry allows me to understand and remember who I was, who I am, and who I can be."

Matthew Burk: "I write poetry because it's a way I can express my feelings with words and let my creativity just flow, turning my feelings into something that people can see as art."

Natalia Chepel: "When I was nine, my family lived in Croatia for two months. It was intended to be a permanent move, but of course things didn't quite work out, so my memory of it is more like an extended vacation—it was so sunny every single day, and we lay on the beach eating frozen yogurt with gummy bears on top. I think that's the greatest I've ever felt in my whole life. I remember this one night, I was left alone for a little bit while everyone was out on a walk, and I just sat down and wrote this poem about my sister. It was about two pages top to bottom, and every line rhymed. I just had this spontaneous feeling, like the best kind of freedom. And I remember my dad's face while he was reading it: he was all sunshine, too. I think about that look more and more often, now, when I'm writing. The thing about poetry is that it can let you go anywhere, and let you talk to anyone. So when I write, and especially when I'm writing poetry, I imagine it's a chance to tell my father about my life again and I'm grateful."

Melissa Alma Di Martino: "Honestly, I don't really write much poetry. I'm glad I wrote this one and I hope people like it!"

Natalie Friis: "I enjoy poetry because it is another art form to read and write. Like music, dancing, and painting, it can almost be considered performing and I love how so much of poetry can be left to interpretation."

Paul Ghatak: "I like to write poems because they are tricky and thoughtful and because they refresh your mind."

Kevin Gu: "I write because the emotions that bottle up within me are too intricate to describe in a linear way. Poetry, specifically, helps me express my stories like the rolling of waves and the uncontrolled flow of water— infinite. Sometimes my writing is purely based on one experience and one emotion, and other times it's an outlet for me to spread important messages that I believe in."

Kakul Gupta: "I realised that poetry is my way to indulge with the world, and I am thankful to my brother for introducing me to it. I love haiku the most, because they are short and succinct. The best thing about a haiku is its juxtaposition: how you are in two worlds in just 3 lines and (less than) 17 syllables."

Maria Gil Harris: "I write poetry to gain a deeper understanding of myself and the thought that comes with it. Through poetry I can explore the many thoughts and ideas like I never could before. Over the past year I have discovered how poetry can be a wonderful outlet to put my thoughts out onto paper. Everything about a poem is carefully thought-out to bring an idea, a story, or a character to life. The literal and metaphorical meanings, the shape of the words in your mouth, the rhythm, even the build of the poem itself. I practice many forms of art, that being music, painting, writing, etc., yet I have never found a better form of expression than poetry."

Adrianna Ho: "I like writing poetry because I can write about anything I like, and also there are many types of poetry. You can be silly when you are writing poetry and you can make it rhyme too! Poetry is the best."

Emma Hoff: "When people read poetry, and literature in general, they finish, and they say, 'I wish that was real.' But in the period of time they read the text, everything in it is real, in a way. I like to write poetry because I like to make unbelievable things real."

Ivy Hoffman: "I don't think there is one answer to why I like to write poetry. In the beginning, I would read poetry to my family and I would wish it was my own. Then, it became a sort of therapy for me. Sometimes I wrote because something was frustrating me and I just needed to work through it. I still find that I discover something new about myself with everything I write, which is the coolest thing, but at this point, I also feel like I am writing simply because it has become such a part of me. It's just like breathing—if you hold your breath for long enough, eventually your body will kick in and start to breathe again. I feel that if I tried to stop writing, after a few days my fingertips would find a keyboard again and before I knew it I would be writing. If you asked me why I love my parents, or my sister, or my cat, I could give you a bunch of things that I love about them, but at the end of the day, those are just traits. I love them because I love them. The same thing goes for poetry. I love it because, well, I do."

Jessie Johnson: "You know that moment when you're so wrapped in a piece of art, so overpowered that chills run across your spine and hours pass in minutes? When there's no need for logical human thought? That, for me, is poetry, and without it, I would think too much and live too little."

Dahee Joy Kang: "When I was younger, the first book that I ever read by myself was Dr. Seuss's *One Fish, Two Fish, Red Fish, Blue Fish*. Now, although I have moved past Dr. Seuss, poetry has become one of my favorite forms of expression."

Chloe Lin: "Poetry is something I turn to when I'm in my head; I've discovered that it's a powerful tool, and it's amazing what it can do for others, as well as yourself. It lets me forget about that essay that's due tomorrow and the petty drama my friends need to tell me about. My hope is that one day, I'll be an inspiration to people like me: lost, but found."

Naomi Ling: "I like to write poetry because it is a medium that can interpret not only creativity, but necessity. Too often do societal and worldly issues go ignored, and poetry is a way to spark conversation."

Josephine Miner: "I like writing songs because it makes me happy and joyful. I like the movement they make you want to do. You can turn anything into a song."

Mackenzie Munoz: "I like writing poetry because it is fun and my mom writes poetry. I want to be like my mom."

Perry Sloan: "I like to be able to express my emotions. I like letting my mind wander and explore."

Hannah Straub: "I like to write poetry because it is an art form that speaks to me and that I identify with unlike any other. Writing poetry has been a way for me to turn my observations and experiences into tangible reflections of how I see the world."

Ha Trang Tran: "I write poetry to find my voice and create something that unifies people."

Shreya Vikram: "Without poetry, I'd waste language. We're lazy more often than not. We speak and write just to acknowledge our mutual acceptance of linguistic and cultural grammar—rather than do the hard work of actual communication. I'm frustrated by how language is used to validate our conformity; how the minute I name an experience, it becomes shared property. How can I put something into words and still let it be mine? What if grammar was just another cliché? What if I didn't trust punctuation rules, dictionary definitions, sentence syntax? Poetry gives you permission to not trust. The poem is unnaming, unlanguage, mine—how could I resist?"

Some poets chose not to include a note.